Thoughts

Jennifer Ollie

Copyright © 2023 A Written Dream, LLC

Published by: Writers Publishing House

Paperback ISBN: 978-1-64873-420-5

All rights reserved. No part of this book may be reproduced in any manner whatsoever without written permission from the author except in the case of brief quotations embodied in critical articles and reviews

Thoughts
A Collection of Love Poems

Jennifer Ollie

Writer's Publishing House

I would like to dedicate this collection of poetry to the dreamers, believers and lovers of love. Never stop believing in yourself, your ability to fulfill your wildest dreams, live in the sun and give more love.

Author's Notes

It is fine to dream and reach beyond the clouds to attain pure love. To share such an experience on a level that is beyond the surface and deeply rooted is possible. These poems represent a mirage of feelings, desires and hopefulness to inspire the reader to not just exist but rather dare to attain the impossible and hold on to true love.

Contents

Taking Flight...1

The Delicate Parts of Me 2

A Heart for Love 3

The Eyes of Love 4

The Heart I Give 9

Smile 10

The Folds of You 11

You...v. 1 12

You...v. 2 13

Goodbye 15

The Enormity of Love 16

Time, Space, Distance 20

It Seems 21

Life In Rear View 22

Black Love 24

Fairy Tales 26

Be inspired 27

Destined 28

Unsent Messages 29

Let Love In 30

Love Under the Moon 35

Tell Me 36

In My Dreams 37

What is love? 38

Existing 41

Giving 42

Rays 44

Holding On 45

The Progression of Me... 46

Write to Be Free. 47

Taking Flight

At night my mind takes flight into creative rhythms of poetry and thoughts that take on their own expression. I guess it's a blessing to be able to share my gift with the world. It's also a blessing to return to something so unique, that ironically serves as a form of therapy. Shedding old things, emerging into the new me. I wonder where it'll take me? Hopefully to see the world, travel to destinations unknown, live a beautiful life outside of my comfort zone. As I daydream on such goals, I think about what it will take to get there, be there and stay there. What will it take to close my eyes and feel totally free?
~ more to come. ♡

The Delicate Parts of Me

The delicate parts of me
Cling to you
My mind, my body and my spirit
Reaches for you
Like the lightest airway of a feather
My heart draws nearer
The look of your eyes paints a perfect picture
A delicate imagery
For what is to come is the unknown
Until then
The delicate parts of me
Hangs on
To the delicate parts of you...

A Heart for Love

If you love someone
Then you're willing to share
Vulnerability, dreams, nightmares and fears
If lasting impressions are all we have
That's how you know that you care
About the well being of the heart
You see yourself in that person
Their spirit
Their touch
True love doesn't ask for much
The encounter stays with you
Days and weeks sometimes months on end
Like the perfect rhyme or melody
True love is blissful and your best friend. ♥

The Eyes of Love

I love you
Even in the perfect storm
I've loved you
The look in your eyes lets me know that love lives right there inside of you
You feel close
You feel whole
You feel like you have been here before
I wouldn't want to dream for a moment of you letting me go
We are connected
Just as trees need branches
And birds need wings
We are connected
A beautiful, enriching kind of thing
This type of encounter may only exist in the movies or maybe once or twice in life

But I'm down to cover you on all sides and exist in the land of no worries because with you I feel it inside...
We are connected
Love is where we reside

"Love Feels Like Pure Air."

The Heart I Give

If I give you my heart
I hope it fills you with purpose
When you close your eyes
And think of me
I hope that it's worth it
If I give you my heart
I hope you will take care of it
I hope that it remains the center of your existence
Don't fumble it
I hope that it makes you look inside yourself
And peel back the layers of hurt and hesitation
Because the heart I give to you
Is just as fragile as your own
Don't break it

Smile

Within a day's work I do think of you
I smile knowing you exist
I smile at the thought of your sweet kiss
I smile knowing we will experience the sun together
I smile at the future
With no empty conversations
No filters
Being in tune with you
Your mind
Your spirit
Taking the road less traveled
I smile
The love, the atmosphere, the possibility
I hold my pillow a little tighter at night
Smiling at the thought of you

The Folds of You

To fit into the folds of you
Allowed me a chance to rest
Perfect puzzle pieces fit
I don't believe I was equipped to withstand when
those pieces were slightly broken
I wasn't prepared to have a hole in my heart
Now I must pick up those pieces
But I don't know where to start
In my mind, there was a point in time when I
daydreamed about the easy parts of you
And when the grooves just fit
It felt like pure solace
I had a chance to exhale
I'm not sure how to move forward
And/or replace it
For now, I'll just remember how it felt fitting into
the folds of you

You...v. 1

I know you
Just as the sun knows the moon
Light knows sound
I know you
And when you inhale your next breath
My heart exhales for you
I move with you
When you're not around
I know what you are going through
I can feel the good and the bad
I'm there to move to the rhythm of you
With the look of love
The mere touch or a kiss
Two souls connected
I will be there to know and love all of you

I love you

You...v. 2

I know you
Just as the sun knows the moon
Light knows sound
I know you
And when you inhale your next breath
My heart exhales for you
I move with you
When you're not around
I know what you are going through
I can feel the good and the bad
I know you
The truths, the lies
The fairytale where my heart resides
I know you
And walking away
Will be such a hard thing to do
Because no matter how many people you'll meet in this life...
There is only one me

And there is only one you

I love you

Goodbye

I never thought I would look love in the face and say goodbye
I never thought the truth would cut so deep
I never lived in reality
Instead, I showed you different parts of me
Placed my hands on top of yours
Closed my eyes
Wrapped myself in thoughts of serenity
Dived into love
I never lived in reality
And I blame me

The Enormity of Love

If love is there to greet you in the morning
How do you adequately take in the experience?
When love smiles at you, does its intensity radiate through your soul?
How does love make you feel?
A special look
An enlighten conversation
A moment in time that reaches far beyond the surface
If you fall deep enough
It becomes a part of you
It's touch
The appeal
The enormity of space it takes
In your everyday thoughts & even in your heart
Love
If it's only with you for a moment
How do you ensure that it stays?

"Where We Reside, Love Is Everywhere."

Time, Space, Distance

Time...
How much do we have
Space...
How many more moments to be shared
Before it ends
How many disappointments will one face
Before you let go
Distance...
Is the road less traveled
The one you will take
Living...
Will you exist in a world
Without your soulmate
Time
Unfortunately, it does end

It Seems

If pure love is something we should all go after then
Why does it seem so far-fetched?
If love presents itself in its' rawest form
Then why do we run away from it?
Hesitation, reservation, insecurity
Are all the things that can hold us back
Back from destiny
Back from radiant dreams

It seems...

As if pure love is unattainable
But don't forget about living and learning
About the work that needs to happen
in between.

Life In Rear View

Just as the sun fades into the night
I will become a distant memory
Driving away from love
There's a photograph of me in your rear view
I hope my experience left you with love, joy and peace
One that you'll never forget
Because what I thought we would become
Is now just a distant memory
I only know one way to be
And the distance you've put between you and me
Hurts
As fog overshadows this short encounter
I hope my eyes stay with you
I hope my moonlight stays with you
I hope I've left you with enough thoughts to stimulate you
I hope my hands held your heart long enough to ignite the very things that touch your soul
As I blow out this candle

I'll cry
But I know why
And I'll just have to live with being your distant memory

Black Love

Black love
Black thought
Black dreams
It's always there to take care of me

We're connected in such a benevolent way
All that matters is us
All that needs to ever show up, is us

I will always give as much as you allow me to receive
And when I say give
I mean all of me
Every moment, every sound, every fiber

Black love…

Soft like the sound of rain
My safe place

The intensity is what will always draw me in

And keep me wanting more...

    Black love is sweet
    Just as it should be.

Fairy Tales

It's fair to say that I dream of fairytales and happy endings. I'm a hopeless romantic in a comfortless world. I know this. But I believe that true love does exist. You know the type of love that doesn't require much, it just fits right in the seat. The type where the air is pure, you can see a solid reflection of yourself. The type that allows you to recline, relax, smile and repeat. Maximum effort on both sides. A supernatural experience, supportive, light-hearted and free. An irresistible yet irreplaceable feeling.
A fairytale scenario.
As much as I believe in its attainability...
In all honesty yet in full transparency
There are times when I don't think it will ever find me.
Until then, I'll just continue to reside in my corner of life and dream about happy endings.

Be inspired

Be inspired to live better
Be inspired to love more
Find your place in the universe to believe...
Believe in your reset, find it in your heart to search
for a deeper meaning
A deeper purpose
Smile
Because how you will be on the other side is
beautiful, transcendent, tall and free
Just simply close your eyes, hold your head back and
imagine yourself breathing, achieving, loving...

A new you.

Destined

I'm destined to fall in love again.
This time love will embrace all of me.
All of my flaws, blemishes and short-comings
It will be gentle with me and take its' time
Love will shower me from my head to my feet
I'll have the freedom to express, freedom to dance, freedom to just…be
I'm destined to fall in love with me
And all of the company and life's riches that come along the way will provide endless smiles and powerful vibrations.
I will lack nothing
Because I am destined to enjoy this ride with no turning back
and filled with great memories.

Unsent Messages

There are so many things I would like to say. So many messages that were meaningful yet went unsent. I wonder if you believe in telepathy because if so then I know we're truly connected. If you can hear my thoughts then please know that I think of you often. I smile at the memories and miss the nature of your voice. If we share the same wavelength then you'll know I hope space and time would return like an orbit. You'll know it if you ever think of me. Because that beautiful smile or those beautiful moments just don't ever fade away. You'll feel it because it's authentic and pure. I hope one day you'll get to hear this message and it won't go unsent.

Let Love In

When love comes, let it enter
Let it bring you peace
Let it wake you up like sunshine
Let it be
Give yourself freedom to express
Relax
Consume pure air
Because my heart will take care of it all
Meet me there
Smile
See yourself in me
I am...love 🖤
Every emotion
Every challenge
Every kiss
Every moment well spent
I am...love 🖤
The way it should really feel

The way life intended

I am...love 🖤
And I love you.

*"Just like the moon and stars,
love is wherever you are."*

Love Under the Moon

Love under a moon is a natural transaction
There's no filter, no airs, no constraints
Just trust
Just us
It's already written
It gives
It radiates
Attaining this level of love is special not difficult
It's just you and I
For all the moments in the future
It holds true
Together
We'll fly under the moon.

Tell Me

Look into my eyes and tell me that you love me. Tell me that you will hold me up in times where I'm weak. Tell me you will restore my energy when I'm on level E. Tell me that you will reach into the sky and rotate the sun just so it shines next to me. Tell me that I am your greatest fantasy. Tell me that I fulfill not just your physical desires but your mind.
Tell me you love me
Tell me you love my soul
Don't look away
Tell.me.that.you.love.me.
Tell me I make you feel whole .
And in return I'll give it all back to you
Every desire, every moment
Everything
Just mean it when you say it
Tell me you love me.

In My Dreams

Today I went to look for you in my dreams
You were there, you never left
You waited for me
And loved my inner soul
You appealed to intellectual senses
Held and healed me
You never went away
We took a long walk
Guards down
It was worthwhile
Then I woke up…
And it was just a distant memory.

What is love?

How should it make you feel?

Well I think it should touch your inner soul.
Be the thoughts that carry you throughout the day.
Be the memories that will last a lifetime.
Love should embrace your failures, flaws and imperfections. Love welcomes your success with open arms. Love should be your peace, an escape, a vulnerable place. It doesn't yell, it's never loud, never belittles, only there to make you smile.

Love should move you, hold you, light you up on the inside. Something that will only help you grow. Provide a deeper meaning towards purpose. A place of safety, the perfect landing space…a march towards eternity. ♥

Existing

What is life if you're only existing?
As days turn into nights
More meaningless moments take up space
No fireworks
No plans
Just going through the motions
It's a tough space to be in
How do you make it to the other side without giving up?
How do you bring back excitement?
How do you do anything more than just exist?

Giving

I want to have everlasting days with you
Laughs that don't end
The ability to see each other's flaws and provide grace from within

I want to fully trust you and fall deeply in love with my head held back free from worry and doubt
Without hesitation
I want us to be aligned but not forced
I want you to wake up everyday and choose me by choice

Honest and accepting of our true selves
Because this is me in the flesh, take it or not
Never-mind how life brought us together because it feels like we can't live apart
I want you to look me in my eyes and see your heart

A safe space
A nurturing place
Take a walk with me
Because I want to give you all that I've got.

Rays

Before I close my eyes to sleep
I thank God for your existence
I thank Him for your spirit
And your sweet, soft kisses

I thank Him for you

You've crawled your way into a space
That was reserved for a special case
And now the days ahead seem to be perfectly colored
with the rays from the sun
Smiles, laughter

And you.

Holding On

The world keeps moving
Leaves turn from green to brown
Life keeps going
But love will always remain constant
And as the sun rises in the morning
So should your dreams
Be. Live. Pursue.
And most of all
Give love to those who love you in return
Hold on to them tight
Because in the blink of an eye
The world keeps moving
All we have is love and each other
Give more

The Progression of Me...

The progression of me believes in my dreams
I believe the sun will shine over the horizon of dark times
It lives
The progression of me is whole yet deep
It breathes
It gives
It looks towards the future
It endures
It takes a walk down a path of the unknown
Heart in one hand, trust in the other
It loves...again

Write to Be Free

I write as a free form of expression
I write to be free
I write to imagine myself in a place
free from fear, worry
or personal insecurities
I write because it's my passion
and destiny
It will always return to me
And I don't doubt myself in this space
I write to fulfill my dreams of peace
and serenity
I write to touch a beautiful life
that will give me reciprocity
and feel my existence
I write to be free.

www.ingramcontent.com/pod-product-compliance
Lightning Source LLC
Chambersburg PA
CBHW072137070526
44585CB00016B/1722